Liz's Little Café

Mary O'Keeffe

One day, Dad said, "Let's go to the **café**. We can get some buns."

"Will **Auntie Liz** be there?" I said.

"Will we get to have some **cakes**?" said Ella.

It was damp and cold, so Dad, Ella and I ran down to the **café**.

There was a hint of **cake** as we went in. Yum!

We sat down at a **table**.

"Let's get a **menu**," said Ella.

Auntie Liz got us all a big mug of hot milk.

Ping! Dad got a text.

"Can you mind Ella and Evan for a little bit?" asked Dad.

"I have to go and pick up some bits for Mam.

I'll be quick."

"Yes," said **Auntie Liz**.

"In fact, Ella and Evan can lend a hand here in the **café**."

Yay! The **café** was only a little busy, but there was a lot to do.

We had to mop and pick up the old cups and mugs.

I had to fill up the jam pots and put the lids on.

Ella put a **menu** on all of the **tables**.

It was fun to do jobs in the **café**.

"Come back here, Ella and Evan! Let's do some buns," said **Auntie Liz**.

She helped us to get all of the bits for the buns.

Ella got the jug of milk.

I got the big pot, the pink pot and the little red pot too.

Auntie Liz got eggs and some zest.

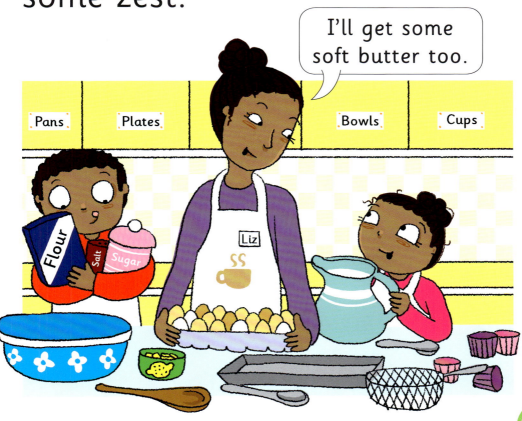

We had to sift, and then mix in the egg and the milk.

"Only put in a little bit from the red pot," said **Auntie Liz**.

"Okay!" said Ella, but she had put in a lot.

It was a lot of salt! Yuck!

"Oh no!" I said.

Ella bit her lip. Uh-oh!

Auntie Liz was not mad.

"Hold on. All is not lost, Evan," she said.

"We can put in some more zest, more milk and more eggs," said **Auntie Liz**.

"They will not be buns.

They will be **pancakes**!

We can get your dad to test them!"

Dad had come back.

He sat down at the **table**.

We gave him one of the **pancakes**.

He began to lick his lips.

"That was so yum!" said Dad.

"I will put Ella and Evan's **pancakes** on the **menu**!" said **Auntie Liz**. "You can help here in the **café** some other day!"